Taking Off

Carmel Reilly
Karen Young

NELSON
CENGAGE Learning™

Australia • Brazil • Japan • Korea • Mexico • Singapore • Spain • United Kingdom • United States

Taking Off

Fast Forward
Yellow Level 8

Text: Carmel Reilly
Illustrations: Karen Young
Editor: Johanna Rohan
Design: James Lowe
Series design: James Lowe
Production controller: Hanako Smith
Audio recordings: Juliet Hill, Picture Start
Spoken by: Matthew King and Abbe Holmes
Reprint: Jennifer Foo

ISBN 978 0 17 012515 4
ISBN 978 0 17 012513 0 (set)

Cengage Learning Australia
Level 7, 80 Dorcas Street
South Melbourne, Victoria Australia 3205
Phone: 1300 790 853

Cengage Learning New Zealand
Unit 4B Rosedale Office Park
331 Rosedale Road, Albany, North Shore NZ 0632
Phone: 0800 449 725

For learning solutions, visit **cengage.com.au**

Printed in Australia by Ligare Pty Ltd
8 9 10 11 12 13 14 21 20 19 18 17

Evaluated in independent research by staff from the Department of Language, Literacy and Arts Education at the University of Melbourne.

Carmel Reilly
Karen Young

Contents

Chapter 1

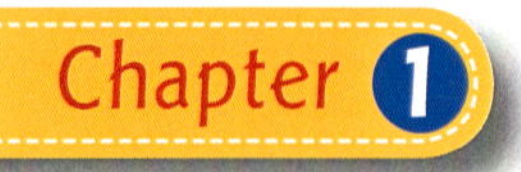

The New Skateboard

Anna jumped on her new skateboard and raced down the hill.

"Hey!" she shouted to some kids who were out on the street. They all turned around as Anna came up to them.

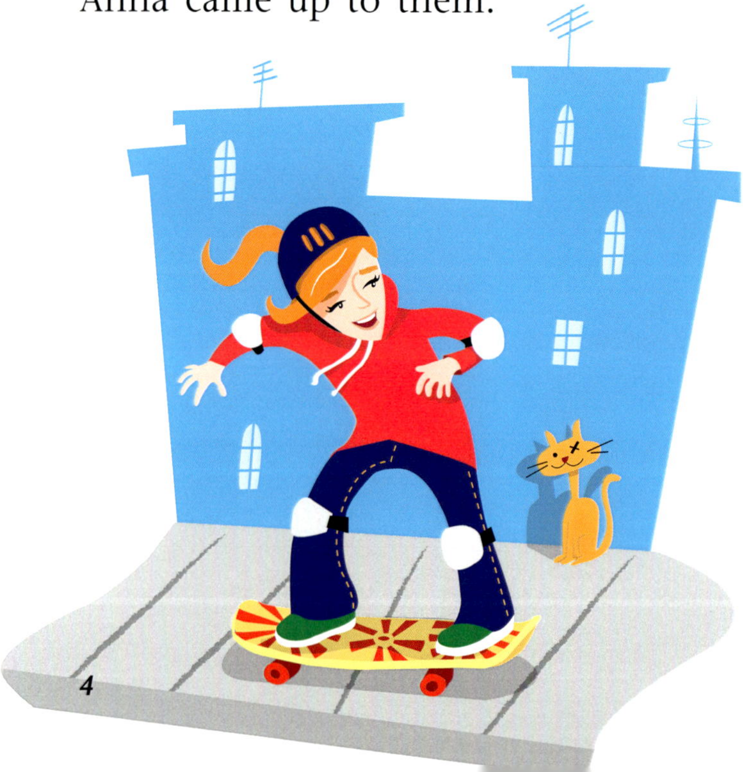

"Cool skateboard," said her friend, Mick, as she stopped.

"Thanks," said Anna.
"I just got it."

Anna picked up her skateboard
and passed it to Mick.
He looked at it and passed it around.

Tom was the last kid to look at it.
He said, "Can I take it for a ride?"

"No," said Anna.
"It's a really, really cool skateboard
and I don't want anything
to happen to it."

"I'm not going to let anything
happen to it," said Tom.
He dropped the skateboard
and put his foot on top of it.

Running Words 126

Chapter 2

Come Back!

Tom really wanted to have a ride.

"Hey," said Anna. "I said 'no'!"

"Oh, go on ..." said Tom,
and he raced off down the street.

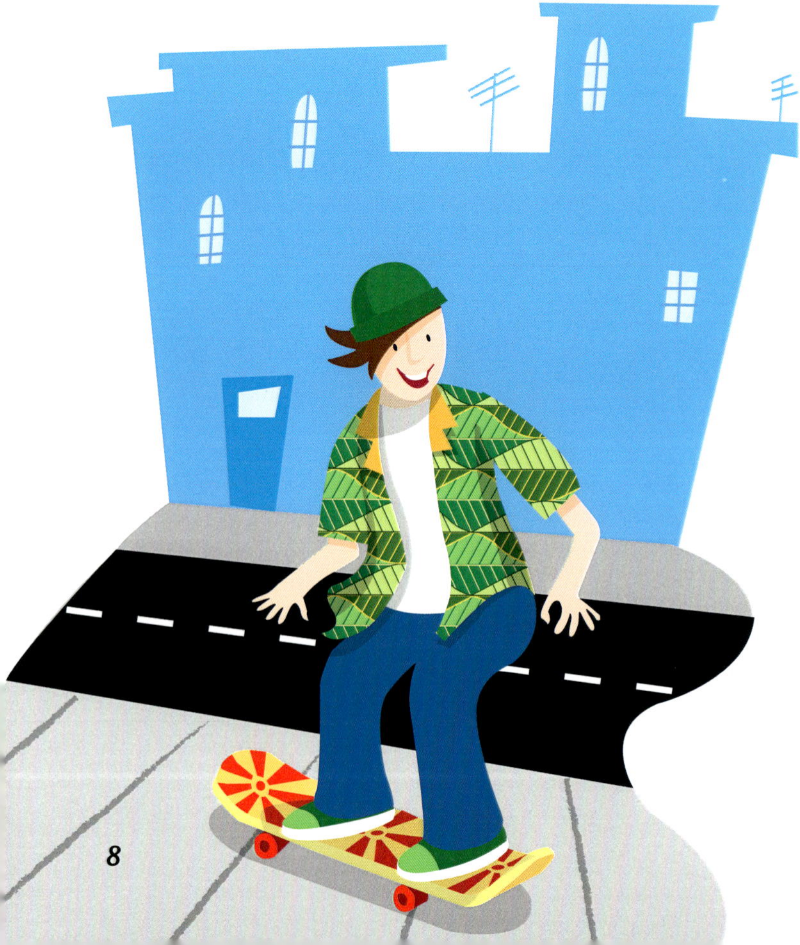

"Come back!" shouted Anna.

"Here," said Mick passing Anna his skateboard.

She grabbed it and raced off after Tom.

Anna could see Tom up ahead.

"Hey! Look out for the bump!"
she shouted.

Tom looked back.
He was shocked to see Anna
behind him.

"Look out!" Anna shouted again.

But it was too late.
Tom went over the bump and fell off.

Chapter 3

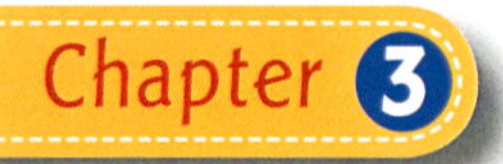

Getting the Money

Tom was sitting on the ground.

"Are you okay?" said Anna, running up to him.

Tom nodded.

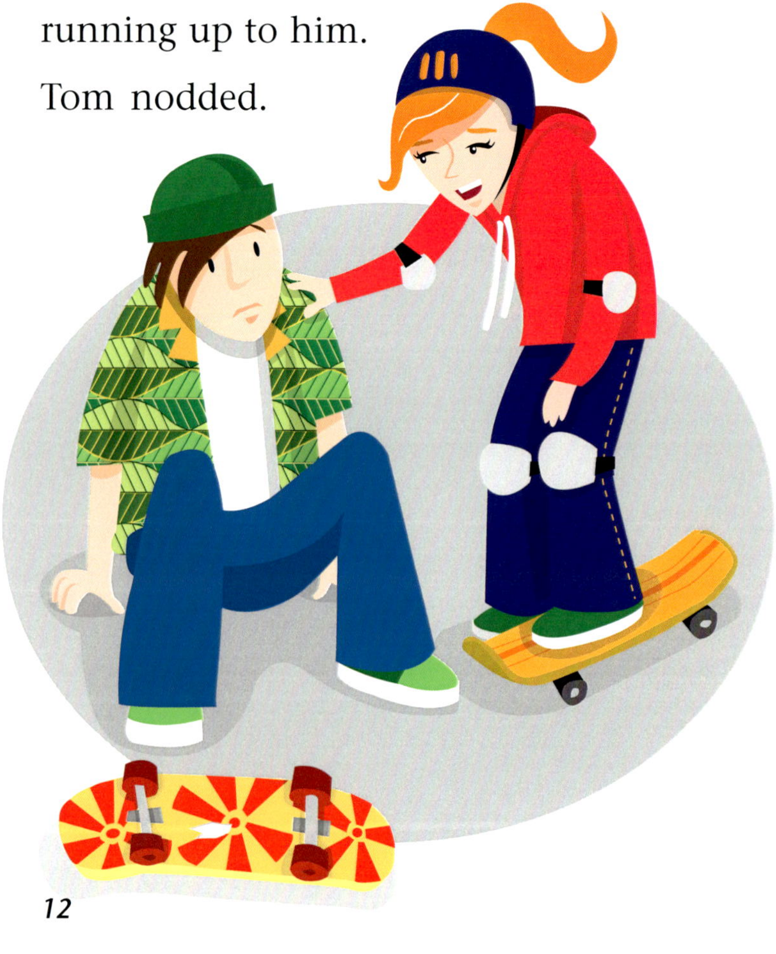

Anna looked at her skateboard,
as Tom was getting up.
A little bit of paint had come off it.

"Why did you take my skateboard?"
said Anna.

"I'm sorry.
I just wanted to have a go.
My mum doesn't have the money
to get me a skateboard," said Tom.

"But you can't take people's things,"
said Anna.

"I'm really, really sorry," Tom said.

"Not all of the money for my skateboard came from Mum and Dad," said Anna. "Most of it came from little jobs I did for people."

"Really?" said Tom.

"Yes, really," said Anna.

Tom looked at Anna.
"Hey, I could do some jobs
to get money, too," he said at last.

"Yes, you could," said Anna.
Then she smiled.
"And, when you get your skateboard,
you can come for a ride with me."

Tom looked shocked,
then he smiled back.
"That would be really good," he said.
"I'd like that a lot."